RUNNING REPAIRS

RUNNING REPAIRS

NORMAN DUGDALE

The Blackstaff Press

British Library Cataloguing in Publication Data

Dugdale, Norman
　Running Repairs
　I. Title
　821'.914　　　　PR6054.U/

　ISBN 0–85640–283–4

© Norman Dugdale, 1983

First published in 1983
by The Blackstaff Press Limited
3 Galway Park, Dundonald, BT16 0AN
with the assistance of
The Arts Council of Northern Ireland

All rights reserved

Printed in Northern Ireland
by Belfast Litho Printers Limited

Καινούριους τόπους δὲν θὰ βρεῖς, δὲν θἄβρεις ἄλλες θάλασσες.
Ἡ πόλις θὰ σὲ ἀκολουθεῖ. Στοὺς δρόμους θὰ γυρνᾷς
τοὺς ἴδιους. Καὶ στὲς γειτονιὲς τὲς ἴδιες θὰ γερνᾷς·

You will not find other places, other seas.
This city will follow you. Through the same streets,
The same neighbourhoods, you will wander and grow old.
                                        C.P. Cavafy, 'The city'

Contents

Theologian	1
Spirit of place	2
Columkille	3
Lent	5
A statement is expected shortly	6
Visitation	7
Pantechnicon	8
End of season	9
Provincia deserta	10
Back to the basics	11
Quis multa gracilis. . .?	12
Souterrain	13
Pillar of society	14
Candles	15
Journeys end	16
Polycrates' ring	17
Michaelmas	18
Home for Christmas	19
Grief	20
Mason	21
How to become an Alexandrian	22
Higher Hodder	23
But for your gifts	25
After the bombing	26
Travelling westward	27
At Saul	28
Scholar in the library	29
Trivia	30
Second-hand bookstall	31
To an English liberal, ten years on	32
Encounters	33

In memoriam G. B. Newe	34
Age	37
Diplomatic reception	38
Shipwrecked mariner	39
Specimen	40
Daybreak	41
Glenarm	42
Small hours	43
Theodotos	44
Running repairs	45
Moralities	46
Silence	49

Theologian

Stooped, blinking at the light, he shambled in,
Lifted up his head, lifted massive paws,
And with hardly a glance at his notes discoursed
For an hour or more. And surely I thought
His mouth was smeared with honey and his huge
Arms crushed the hushed hall to his breast
In clumsy tenderness. But next to me
A young girl screwed her mouth into a yawn,
Fingered her bracelet, raised a hand to smooth
Her cascade of bright hair. In blood's blind jig,
The dream of flesh engrossed, why should she
With this gaunt old man hunger for discarnate truth?

Spirit of place

These days I know you only
By your absences, the landscape
Empty and inert: or when,
Still nowhere to be seen, you nonetheless

Look coldly on me, intruder
On your lonely dance at noon,
Transgressor of your woods and streams,
Your pastures and your drumlins.

It was not always so. Once,
Furze crowned the rounded hills,
Gold chaplets of your bravery;
Your banks hid snowdrop, primrose,

Violet. I dipped my hands
Into the rills, and felt your touch
Like cool silk on me: all your weathers
Running through my flesh like fire.

Columkille

I

The mountains sprang to guard his birth,
Bald sentinels, their molten wars
Transfixed for ever in arrest of rock;

Or wheeling at full gallop froze,
White manes flying in the wind,
To flank him from the sea. For him

Salmon crammed the sound by night
Between Horn Head and Tory
To flail upstream and thud at dawn

About his feet. Beside his stead
The blackbird sang on spangled thorn
And honeysuckle in the hedges

Twined with pale dog-rose to weave
Him coronets of sleep. Among
The shadows of God's plentitude

The eagle soared. What hurled him then
Headlong, the great breast stormed, his pinions
Scattered in the eye of risen sun?

II

Now, nothing's left but legends and a few
Stones standing in the windy west. Year by year
I come to track him and interrogate
The sole remaining witness – a bony hag
Tricked in a torn green skirt. Too many ghosts
Ramble among her memories. She dreams
Of youth and an imagined rape
Committed on once lovely limbs, of wild geese

Swallowed in the storm, of ships
With human cargo starving in their holds
Among the rats and cholera. I piece
The tale together. Some of it makes sense.
The rest is maundering, not evidence.

Suppose her foul mouth, though, and riddling tongue
Speak oracles? Suppose that tripod stool,
The spittle drooling from her lips, her knotted hair
And staring eyes are mantic? My lot came
To plant and build and to possess, sweeping
Down from Derry, pragmatic in their phlegm:
But could not read the omens then
And will not now. The English vice, it seems,
Is not hypocrisy but cosiness,
A bland refusal to admit extremes
Whether of evil or of holiness –
As if good manners, charm and chintz
Could tame the tiger at the gate or win
To household tricks the beast within.

III

What shimmers through the golden haze?
No dove, an eagle towering in the sun,
That gaunt figure with the staff
And beaked, square head and burning eyes
Advancing with the symbols of his wrath.

I stare again. Shadows reel
Across the bog. On flat-backed Muckish cloud-scud
Skims, and darkens. White-pointed Errigal
Bursts the sodden bag of rain, and all
Vistas vanish as the land

Runs westward with its decks awash
Pitching into winter. We cling to spars
And cordage, drowning in the common night
Of history with that warrior-saint
Engulfed, who stumbled once towards the light.

Lent

East by north all winter through
Wind dropped at last, hoarfrost thick
On bole and bank, the ponds
Glazed over, songbirds silent. Only

The whins fought back, burnished shields
Embushed by the wayside, flaring
In the smouldering red dusk
Of ice-bound days. Then, at winter's end,

This sudden turbulence,
Tormenting the stripped trees'
Arthritic limbs, flattening
Pelt and fur, flings hail, rocks mind

From moorings, scatters me like straw.
They give no ground though, ever,
Barbaric in their splendour
Of Mycenaean gold: beset by thorns

Burst through now to resurrection.

A statement is expected shortly

Thrace devastated now, the barbarians
Are marching, it is rumoured, on the Capital,
Their vanguard raising thunderclouds of dust.
Already, looters fire the suburbs, and carts
Piled high with household goods and children
Jostle through the gates. In the foreign quarter
A disaffected rabble stones the guards,
Screaming abuse. The Emperor is aghast.
He weeps before the Council, whose members
Have dispatched an embassy with gifts
For the barbarian king, and a dignified
Remonstrance in faultless Attic prose
Which hints at subsidy: though the Treasury,
In fact, is empty. They sigh.
There is nothing more to be done. Meanwhile
It is important to keep up appearances.
Perhaps the Empress Mother may be moved
To admonish her son. She at least believes
In the miraculous intervention of the Virgin.

Visitation

I recognised first the gesture,
Then the voice, and then
The glance of sunlight on your hair
Swept back like a raven's wing. So,
Even before you turned towards me,
My heart knocked in its cage
And I dropped my gaze lest my eyes
Be scorched by your presence.
When I looked up again
You were gone: not to be found
In the weary crowds, shuffling here
Through dust and stones and heat.

Pantechnicon
for Padraic Fiacc

This thing goes faster and faster. Brakes worn,
Tyres frayed, the steering wobbly and the road
Dropping ahead, the whole contraption
Jolting, rattling, lurching under its load

Is bound to crash soon. But look through the mirror
Behind, and the past moves in slow motion
Like a cricket-match in a sunlit field, or
Stands frozen in mid-gesture, figures on

A marble frieze – the perspectives all foreshortened,
Your friends, your loves still in their prime, smiling
So that you might turn to greet them, mend
The foolish quarrels, threads snapped in the dark labyrinth

Of time: or would if you weren't bucketing downhill,
Scared to death and hanging onto the wheel.

End of season

Like a playful smack on a barmaid's bottom
The flood tide slaps and fondles the sea-wall
In summer while the world strolls by.

But see what the ebb, this winter afternoon,
Reveals: broken bottles, condoms, cans, the green
Dribble of a rusty sewer.

And only the old are left here now
With gulls for company, red-beaked scavengers
Screaming in the bitter wind.

Provincia deserta

Well, here it is: not Botany Bay
But a penal settlement all the same,
The sentence life without remission – saving,
Of course, Sir, such as yourself, gentlemen newly come
To live here at the Governor's Lodge. Two years from now
You will be safely home again and dining out
On your bizarre experiences, which cannot fail
To please your hostess and amuse the company.

Let me then briefly sketch our way of life. First,
Custom binds us, hardly ever law. Mating,
Which takes the mind off other things,
We openly encourage, especially
For procreation: but only, note, within each tribe.
(Exogamy means instant ostracism.)
Condemned at birth, children are consigned
By parents to our priests for prompt initiation
In rituals of wrath, the wine of vengeance.
All punishment is random and condign, each
Adult male doubling as both predator
And victim – a symbiosis which ensures
All suffer in the end alike. Please don't be
Alarmed, though. Well-trained squads clean up the carnage
And maintain tolerably hygienic conditions
For temporary survivors.

                                      You find this strange,
No doubt; and stranger still our fierce
Cleaving to the only thing
We share and murder for. It is a land,
You see, of quite surpassing beauty,
Of stream and mountain, lake and wood
With many haunting presences

Which will shadow you always, beckoning
Still, however far your country.

Back to the basics

Here we go again: pulse, temperature,
Blood tests, blood-pressure, samples of urine,
X-ray, electrocardiogram. Any
Chest-pain, shortness of the breath? How soon,
Old hands or new, we settle to the strict routine
Of their impersonal compassion.
O yes – and here's the motherly old hen,
Convalescent now, who clucks about the ward
In her dressing-gown, comforting the lonely
Or the shy; who always has a reassuring smile
For anxious visitors at the next bed;
And used to being useful, helps the hard-
Pressed nurses hand out early morning tea.

Quis multa gracilis . . . ?

Short back-and-sides, I slump into a chair
Vacated by a long-haired youth,
And dodging what the mirror shows me stare
At a slogan on the wall. 'Better For Both',
It says, picturing a tall, bronzed man, coat slung
Across his shoulder, right arm round
His laughing girl, leading her through summer fields
Towards a copse. Shampooed now, back-combed, scent-sprayed,
The young on either side hitch up their jeans
And go, toileted for Aphrodite
Whose wares augment this barber's trade.

I think of the Spartans at Thermopylae
Preening themselves for death. But history
Is silent elsewhere on the way
They coped – no pill, no sheath, visiting their girls
By stealth. Better for both? Who knows? Probably
The same old sorry human mess, I'd say.

Souterrain

I wonder about this Macedonian
Painted in his pomp, his Asian triumphs
Fresh still in the public mind, by Hermes now
Wafted towards the seat of judgement. Surely
Distinguished service overseas to king
And country should settle matters in his favour
Once for all – the exigencies of war
And, here or there, a little indiscriminate
Slaughter notwithstanding. (A wise general
Must learn to give his troops their head at times.)
Besides, from all he had heard his judges too
Were gentlemen, devoted to blood-sports
In their day, and horses, drink and women.
If not, he could always bully and bawl
At them like raw recruits on his parade-ground
At Pydna long ago.

                    But do I detect
A slight unease beneath his arrogance,
A certain faltering of stride? Let me
Salute him then in this windless place,
The sense of failure settling like fog
On both of us, met here beside the path
That winds through reeds and marshland, its cold
Silence chilling the mind, acrid in the mouth.

Pillar of society

Yes, he hankered for respectability
All right, accumulating honours. But
To his womenfolk at least he must have been
A trial to live with, finicky and glum
Never satisfied with what he'd got,
Fancying himself indeed – at his age
Too, silly old cod – with high-born ladies
And craving fresh infatuation.
And all the while, out of the weed-grown past
And walled-off gardens of his mind in autumn
He plucked his golden fruit. The whole performance
Was ridiculous. But then the muse takes lodging
Where she will: this ancient in his dotage,
That dowdy, ill-used woman in her grave.

Candles

I have lit candles for you all through Greece
In censed cool silences, golden gloom
Out of the heat and glare; in dusty shrines
Of disused monasteries foundering
Beneath wistaria and clematis,
The rust-green drag of barnacled decay;
In chapels perilous among the mountains
Where lost Byzantium's faint afterglow

Illumines last hieratic gestures, spells
Against the dark. The mysteries burn within
Of the crucified god, anguish of love,
Of loss. Beyond, spread scents of thyme and tamarisk,
White townships cascading to waterfronts,
Horizons of the purple-stained Aegean.

Journeys end

Expresses glide now into termini; screws
Threshing astern, ferries inch towards quays;
And whistling jets thump down on runways, roar
Suddenly and trundle to a stop. All void

Their passengers into the city's maw
Where other travellers wait
In lounge-bars or in crowded cafeterias
Among beer-stains, baggage, cigarette stubs, tea

Slopped in saucers, for trains or planes or buses.
Humanity's endemic mess apart,
These migrations mostly serve some end
Of public gain or private profit. A few

Are blessed, in the pale March sun
Bringing together separated lovers
Across great continents or estuaries
To ease them of their ache.

Polycrates' ring

My brother of Egypt counsels me
Concerning my wealth and state: 'To avert
The envy of the gods, rid yourself now
Of your most precious possession.' Well,
I have done as he says: have cast my gold
Signet-ring into the sea, the symbol
Of my selfhood, a thing of exquisite
And cunning workmanship, set with sapphire,
Emerald, amethyst.
                    The soothsayers and priests
Applaud my perspicacity. Thus to appease
The gods, and yet be rich and powerful still
Belongs, they tell me, to the highest statecraft.
I am undeceived, for no man can discard
His inmost self, even by proxy. But
They are right to rub their hands, these flatterers,
And smile and nod, with talkative anticipation
Gathering for my feast. Not for them the faint
Ironic laughter on Olympus,
The Persian's guile, the derision of history.

Michaelmas

Above a shining sea honeysuckle
Flares now through the hedgerows. By bank, by ditch
Bright with campions and foxgloves, bees
Weave their delicate dance, and purple vetch

Hangs tremulous. Others will pass this way
In just such weather after we have gone,
Years hence. But never a sweeter day,
Blackberries swelling in the sun,

Will they know than this: such sharp delight
As ours, stepping here towards the night.

Home for Christmas

The people I encounter in the street
Have hardly changed. Pinched by cold, eyes dulled
By small defeats, mouths thin drawn
Less in bitterness than resignation,
They are cumbersome and patient as slow cattle.
Yes, I have seen them all before. But then
They belonged to my parents' generation,
Now to mine – done for, like this raw
And windy town among the Pennines, stone-faced
Still, although its looms stopped long ago.

Grief

Slow as slugs the lines
Of limousines and mourners stretch,
Contract, and crawl to the graveside
Or crematorium. A snatch of psalm: then
The prayer for the committal. . . in sure
And certain hope of resurrection. . .
Is blown down-wind or drifts like smoke
Above grey heads. All's over
Bar the burning, or the knock
Of earth on wood.
                      In canopied twilight
Across the fields of summer far away
Gasping lovers twine in ecstasy –
Their puny evanescent cries
Fading in the silences of sea
And night and stars.

Mason
for John Hewitt

That I read your verses always on some train
Or plane, or lying high and dry in hospital
Is wholly by choice, not accident. For travel
Or sickness clears the mind of the quotidian,
Clears the sight, so that a man can see
The chiselled lettering, the polished grain,
Your shaping hand at work on native stone,
The practised eye through seven decades
Lithomantic, measuring innate form.

How to become an Alexandrian

You lecture in English. This confers prestige
(It is better to lecture than to teach)
And creates a presumption of knowledge.

There are other advantages – short hours,
Long holidays, security of pay
And tenure, a captive audience

Of the impressionable young. What's more,
You can display as much aggression
And look as scruffy as you please

On or off the job. In no time at all
You will be asked to parties, will appear
On platforms to prolonged applause

For your courageous stand against oppression
At home here or abroad. You might – who knows? –
Be seen some off-peak evening on the telly,

Crammed bum and belly into crotch-tight jeans,
By far the hairiest of the panel
Of show-biz tarts and talkative old queans.

Higher Hodder

On Hodder Bridge I pause to map
Under its slow white sail of cloud
The full-rigged landscape freighted now
With summer's load. Trout slide,
Slim shadows, into dark green pools
Below. At matins in the grass
Crickets chirr their dry descant
Shrilly on the dale's deep murmur.
My grandfather at eighty fished this stream
Walking the green heart still of grace
On mornings like this morning thick
And drowsy with the musk of may.

Like holm-oaks gripping ground they grew,
Stone by knuckled stone, the gnarled
Arthritic villages – Chipping,
Slaidburn, Whitewell, Downham, Mitton –
Pitched in a pentagram askew
About this spot. Silting slow
In time, their musty churches fly
Crossed banners still against oblivion.
But how can that frail figure stay
The worm within; or bell-tower bind
That counts instead the silent loss, drip
By drip, of the leaking world's life-blood?
Demdike and Chattox in my father's day
Were names to scare a child: witches creaked,
Wild geese across the moon. A stricken
Paradise it must have been
Which luckless generations fled
To fill the rumbling bellies of the mills
Famished for their flesh – snuffed wick
Smouldering by night beyond the hills,
All fire, all freshness poisoned to the quick.

Strange, then, how this broad dale tugs
The mind at farthest reach – through sheer
Salt weather homing, fog, an ice-fanged sea –
To tether it at last. Now
I catch my hands in middle-age
Making my father's gestures, mark them
His hands upon the rough warm stone
At rest, stiffening here while sun
Bursts seed and all the crescent year
Burns to June's core. I grow these days
Downwards, back into the moil
Of masticating earth. Among
Old bones, old boulders, stumps of rotten tree
The blind roots clutch and curl; and ways
Not my ways knurl my trunk, bend, slowly master me.

But for your gifts
from the Greek of Nicephoros Brettakos

But for your gifts, Lord, of poetry
What should I have to live on now?
These fields would not be mine:
Whereas I rejoice here in my apple-trees,
Rejoice that my stones have fructified,
That my cupped palms fill with sunlight,
My desert with people,
My garden with nightingales.
And what do you think of them, Lord? Have you seen
My sheaves of corn? Have you seen my vines?
How pleasant is the light that falls
On my sheltered valleys?

And I still have time.
I have not yet cultivated all my land.
Pain clears my plot, ploughs me deeper still.
I scatter my laughter like shared bread, yet
I do not spend your sun improvidently,
I do not let fall even a crumb of what you give me:
Because I am mindful of the storms of winter,
Of the nightfall soon to come. Before I go
I must make my hut a church
For the shepherds of love.

After the bombing

Between the fire-tongued shells of warehouses
And boarded-up shop windows, hand in hand,
They came hurrying down the street, laughing
Together and smiling at each other,
Then paused at the kerb to snatch a kiss
Before stepping across the road still strewn with glass
And vanishing down an alleyway – so
Blithe, so radiantly swift
Their passage that it swung the mind away,
The needle oscillating those few seconds
From hate's dead reckoning.

Travelling westward

Travelling westward this day through the shires,
Worcestershire, Gloucestershire and Somerset,
Timbered, cricketing counties tinged with leaf
And blossom in the first faint flush, the stir

Of summer's deep, slow music, I think
Of that farther island in the west,
Her famished fields, whins lighting the loanings,
Stony acres slashed with seams of gold.

I should have left her long since, settled here
Where I belong. Not now. What should I do
Without her, soft-tongued, virginal-seeming
Slut that she is? I have grown old

In her toils, her meltings and evasions,
The narrow quarrel of our fruitless bed.

At Saul

Rouse me, March, from this long torpor
Now daffodils at muster blow
Their bugles in the dells and whins
Break cover in the gullies, roar
Up bank and boreen, fire drumlins,
Set byres ablaze, with ragged rush
Of spike and banners swarm below
To storm townlands where shrubs in ambush

Shell-burst, showering gold. Then shake
Me, March, out of my lethargy.
With shrill of wind in wire, earth's strum
And stress, your prologue mounts. Soon thunder-crack
Of riven rock shall split the tomb
And wild sap shoot in the dead Tree.

Scholar in the library

A flash of legs and high heels past his desk
Diverts his ageing eye (discreet perfume, neat
Blouse and skirt, a trim hair-do), lust's surge
And sudden sharp constriction gripping groin
And throat. Sensing this, she turns and smiles,
Frailer, older, sadder than she had seemed
At first from the rear view. What now? Should Bacchus
Leap upon astonished Ariadne, or
Subside behind his books to hide his shame?

Trivia

Crowning these hills, a knot of roads
Drawn tight, unsignposted, snaking here
Through hedgerows: glimpses of sea,
Dark headlands dwindling down the coast;
A shining lough, and mountains
Criss-crossed, netted by the morning sun;
A carious city muttering below
Under the smoke-haze. I halt
Among my contradictions
Warming myself meanwhile against the blaze
Of fuchsias this autumn day. Deeper
Than doubt, more ancient than my tongue can name,
There are powers here hobbling choice. Which way to turn?

Second-hand bookstall

In the photograph that forms the frontispiece
He stands by Priam's wall, screwing up his eyes
Against the sun, a smiling, slightly built
Young man, not unlike the former Prince of Wales
Travelling in those days incognito
In baggy shorts that reached down to his knees.
The date: April 20th, 1939.

Leafing through his verses now, I see that they
Were dedicated to the King (no less)
Of the Hellenes, their preface by a Head of House
At Oxford – distinguished auspices indeed.
Yet his book, alas, was still-born, filled
Only with nostalgia for the ancient world
But void of suffering or sense of loss.

And anyway, what sort of fist would he
Have made of Troy, I wonder, among the flies
And stink and sweat, the muscle-bound, vainglorious
Louts, the sodomy and rape and slaughter?
In the library at Alexandria now
He might have sat at ease among his kind.
But with scowling Achilles and all that gang?

Still, I shall keep the book. Not by design
But inadvertence it reveals another world
Gone under – of strolling parasols
And blazers through the leisured afternoon
Loitering by river-banks, and croquet
On the lawn, and hand-bells tinkling for tea:
Of England's late Edwardian dream

The final flowering.

To an English liberal, ten years on

They bomb and burn and slaughter still. 'Why yet?' you cry.
The Saxon raped their Mother-goddess.
They want revenge. To hell with your redress.
How else now can they prove their potency?

Encounters

Some are by fate, not accident.
You know them not by reckoning the odds
Against coincidence of time and place.
(The statistics of probability
Will teach you nothing.) You know them by
Your shaking heart, the shock of recognition
And shiver in the presence of the numinous.
They are exalting but terrible. And one
May be enough to haunt a lifetime.

In memoriam G. B. Newe
from Clinical notes, 1972
'leti discrimina parva'

A staff nurse through the sleeping ward
Rustles like a sigh. Tonight my mind
Runs calm and clear: runs all on you,
Old friend, lonely in your distant glen
And vilified by your own kind.
What comfort can I give you then?
I picture you, beside a great turf fire
Reading late or dozing in your chair
While the North Atlantic gasps outside
And gripes through its black gullet from Kintyre
To Benmore Head.

                You knew the cost
Of not stampeding with the rest
Or hurling a bomb or abuse
Was ostracism at the best —
At worst, a bullet in the back.
But 'Charity comes first,' you said,
'Not justice. Justice without charity
Will never reconcile or make us whole.'

Well, those words were mouthed into the gale
And torn away. Against such odds
As faced you for a lifetime none
But a fool would so persist, or one of God's
Own saints — only to see the politics
Of outrage and atrocity prevail.

I've no comfort, then, for you,
Only reasons for despair. Besides,
What's left for you or me to do –
So brittle are the fictions now
That shield us from death's truth – except
To write our memoirs while we may?
'My God, no. Not yet,' you'll say.
'For after charity come faith and hope,
Not self-justification. And anyway,
I've no choice. The work goes on because it must,
And will, long after I am dust.'

I'm not so sure; and yet it comforts me
This pitching night flecked by the spume
And slobber of the maniacal sea
To know the candle shines still in your room.

II
Cushendall, 1982

Ten years ago I wrote that verse
But neither named or sent it to you then.
(The times were out of joint and both of us,
For different reasons, on the danger-list,
Though both of us survived.) Now,
Your throaty chuckle stopped and sideways smile,
You have gone into the world of silence
And I am here this sharp November day –
The sea dead-calm, cold sunlight on the headlands –
To pay my last respects beside your grave.

This was your place, and these your people
Who welcome me, a stranger to their rite,
With rough warm handshakes bonding common grief.
The life you shared with them of cult and creed,
Throb and pulse-beat of the hidden force,
Far older even than your faith, which stirs
In rock, in spring, woodlands of the streaming glen,
I could not touch or share. I knew you
Only as you moved about the world
Beyond these hills, a quiet man
Whose quiet courage and humility
Moved mountains in your time, left fallen humankind
Astonished by its own propensity
For good.

       Never again, this next spring or the next,
Will you see the glens blaze out in glory.
The flame you lit – scholar, mercy's agent
And historian, at rest in your own earth –
Gutters in the wind, your shielding hands
For ever now withdrawn. Swinging here
From doubt to hope, from hope to doubt again,
I turn away, into the rising gale,
Storm-clouds scudding on the peaks, the lash of rain.

Age

Is the dead patch of the skin that pricked
Yields no sensation

The dry cells of the brain where memory
Has withered at the root

The slag and clinker of a heart gone cold
As body shrinks

Into the posture of the womb again,
Craving warmth.

But most it is the rage
Within of folly and desire, impotence

A hunger-striker
Rattling in vain its gaunt contracting cage.

Diplomatic reception

Drinks in hand they bellow
At each other through the smoke
Like rival rugby packs confused
About their code. The sheer

Bulk and hairy mass
Of their sweating masculinity
Tramples me under in the ruck. I vanish,
A Cheshire cat behind my smile

Watching them kick and bite and claw
And scramble for advantage. But suppose
I stumbled some night into your chamber,
Queen, a scullion with sullied shift

And greasy brow. Would you too
Ignore me, nullity
Who even in your private presence,
Crouched at your knee, is never seen?

Shipwrecked mariner

That sea-cleft, shadowed coast drew him unaware
Of sudden darkness, storm and reef. Pitched ashore,
He staggered to the clearing where –
Its fragrant wood-smoke drifting through the trees –
Her palace lay. And there for sure she paced
The terrace in the evening light, her hair
Unbound, her handmaids all dismissed,
As if expecting some Odysseus.
What then to do – spring forward, clasp her knees
Mastering her spell? No. To mingle with the goddess
Was not, he knew, for such as him. Must lie
That night and every night
Among the acorns with the grunting swine,
Lost companions in the witch's sty.

Specimen

Where has it gone, that gift
In childhood and youth of concentration
Which nothing almost could disturb? I would fall
Into contemplation like a saint
In a trance: but of things profane –
Some toy or book, a game or a girl – while,
Beyond, the dingy town trudged by in drizzling rain.

Now, when I should fix my thoughts
On my end, repenting all I have done
And not done, repairing what I can, my mind
Wanders, a butterfly by every breeze
Wafted from shrub to flower, from flower to stone
In the sun staggering for scent or warmth. Then
I am gone again, for some fresh chapel of ease

Or wayside shrine at random.
Bees gather honey for the hive, but I
Only brush my world, each passing moment
Mourning the past, with nothing won,
No store, no foothold. Transfix me, then, content
To loiter thus through summer: who from
My chrysalis failed somehow to emerge as man.

Daybreak

As, in a silent town, life stirs
Before the dawn, and lights flick on
In curtained rooms at random, so

Wakening, I tiptoe round
Your sleeping form and lift the blind
On empty streets. Like dew

This crystalline, still moment
Hanging here: will tremble, fall,
Fracture with the onrush of the day.

Glenarm

Ageing man, I walk the lanes alone
At twilight in this northern latitude
Mid-summer cool as ever, rags and clots
Of rain-cloud scattered in the west,
While down below a cold grey sea
Slaps the headland, heaves
And drags its bulk along the shore.

Yet see, honeysuckle flowers again, twined
In hedges with dog-rose. It pierces the heart,
Such brief brave beauty fading in the dusk:
Frail as love, foundering
In suck and slobber, downdrag of the dark.

Small hours

Coming back from that long journey
Is always the same — always night, clouds
Scudding across the moon, rain-squalls
Bouncing off the tarmac, a big wind

Out of the heave and slop
Of the weltering Atlantic
Shoving the car crabwise
As you cross the dark plateau. Then

Suddenly the cratered city
Opens below, glittering there
Like a gigantic jewelled drinking-bowl,
And you slither down to find

Its doors slammed shut, blinds drawn
Against the stranger, its streets deserted
Though traffic-lights blink madly at road-ends.
And always you feel you are being watched

From alleyways and corners, stalked
As you halt or hesitate
Within the maze. Next day
You recognise the place as home,

Crumpled, mud-stained and familiar
As some old suit, camouflage
Which only half conceals from mind and eye
The sub-culture of murder and atrocity

Flourishing below. And you pick your way again
Warily with thousands more through one
Of history's less successful side-shows:
Best left, the archeologists will say,

Its docklands derelict, its last tides ebbed,
As salt-marsh to the sea-birds, or to silence.

Theodotos
after Cavafy

Consider carefully, you who belong
To the truly elect, consider now –
However great your glory, your triumphs
In Italy and Greece, however powerful
Your partisans in Rome, or numerous
The honorific titles and addresses
Voted by ancient cities – consider
How you have achieved your eminence.

And you, whose life seems so pedestrian,
Monotonous, respectable, obscure,
Don't count on your complacency, don't think
That nothing frightful will be dredged up from your past.

Remember Theodotos, who is always lurking
Somewhere in the crowd, ready to elbow forward
With Pompey's staring head, its severed grin
Confronting you upon the dismal platter.

Running repairs

'It won't be much of a job, you understand –
Simply a makeshift minor op.
Under a local anaesthetic. Certainly
Things won't be any worse, and given luck
They should be better. A proper job, of course,
Would not only take much longer but
Would call for general anaesthesia
Which is not recommended in your case.'

Not recommended in my case. . . ? H'm, old
Bangers can't be choosers, I suppose.
And anyway it isn't far from here
To the knacker's yard. 'Oh, very well, then: just
So long as you can keep me on the road.'

Moralities

I

Given that human nature gravitates
Always towards the worst, what is to be done?

Strangle the instinctual man, he may
Turn briefly blue but won't stop kicking.

Age brings no cure. It banks the fires;
Craves, more than youth, a bestial ecstacy

Though that is not the worst. Lust at least
Implies relationship, which sometimes

(God knows how) may flower into love.

II

First, merely a donkey's distant bray, the harsh
Honk of the quotodian disturbing

The murmur of an August afternoon
And adolescence dreaming in the sun

Then, with middle age, mephitic, slovenly
Familiar, appropriating bed and board,

Failure settles down to a life-tenancy,
Squats there grosser by the day, to jeer

At body's decay, while outside on the sands
Of summer the young display triumphant flesh

To mark mind's slow, insistent drip, its concentration
Leaking like a tap, to pick the sore

Of being passed over, leap-frogged
By lesser men, or worse, by better

The opportunities foregone for ever,
The blunders all now irretrievable

And love betrayed. For stealing fire
From heaven, vultures tore Prometheus

On the far Caucasian rock. Remorse,
The too-late dawning of self-knowledge

Hanged Judas.

III

God's dead, they say. Old Nobodaddy's done for,
Gone for good, an unnecessary hypothesis –

And therefore not susceptible to proof
One way or the other. But what's for sure

Is that the deadly old gang keep
Their sevenfold cunning, briskly work the crowd

Like tipsters, con-men, tarts on Derby Day,
Their pickings rich as ever: with nudge and wink

Fuel ancient fantasies of flesh
And power, or feed anxiety. Yet

After the fun, what's left behind among
The beer-cans, bottles, bits of paper

Which damp gusts strew on trampled grass,
Is a litter of disappointed hopes,

An odour like the faint, stale
Smell of smegma under the prepuce.

IV

The worst
Is to be humped off pick-a-back by Self

(That mis-shaped minor devil in the play
With strong, foul stink and flaysome grin

Who leaps on stage to grab his own
In smoke and thunder of the final act)

And dumped then in the midst of desolation,
Utterly alone, where there is neither beast

Nor birdsong, no leaf, no shade, no water,
And no redemption save

Through the miraculous daring
(Is it only a mirage,

The flickering horizon?)
Of the frail, unbidden dove.

Silence

We have quarrelled before, and parted. But
Even as she flounced out, slamming the door,
I knew I should come home some day to find
Her repossessing her abode, the rooms
Filled suddenly with light again and laughter.

Not this time, though. This time
There were no high words, only the scowl
And scorn of her averted face. Stale smoke,
Slopped tea, an unmade bed: I frowst here
In the gloom, half-hoping still the phone might ring.

*Poetry from
The Blackstaff Press*

JOHN HEWITT
Loose Ends

Respecting trust and personality, relishing language and idiom, these new poems gain, apparently without effort, insights into society, art and self. Writing about the countryside, the city and the 'troubles', John Hewitt is precise, lucid, compassionate and loving, part of 'life's bright process'.

0 85640 284 2   £3.95

Kites in Spring

In John Hewitt's much-praised sonnet sequence about his Belfast boyhood, echoes of the outside world – the sinking of the Titanic, the Young Citizen Volunteers in Belfast – mingle hauntingly with the gentle sounds and small pleasures of a loving family life.

'Here is that unusual book – a book of verse which – hard to believe, I admit – holds the reader's attention from start to finish. . .'
– Paul Durcan
0 85640 206 0   £3.95

Mosaic

'Seldom since Yeats has an Irish poet been gifted with a defter touch, an ability to pen such energetic lines.' – *Irish Press*

'The best of Hewitt in *Mosaic* is what it has always been; and he defines it himself in the poem 'Style': 'a slow measured art/irrevocably plain', put to its best use in evoking and recollecting the Ulster landscape and its people, and in such historical vignettes as 'The Curfew Tower', a poem which suddenly, towards its close, explodes – *Times Literary Supplement*

0 85640 253 2   £3.50

Poetry from
The Blackstaff Press

ROY McFADDEN
The Selected Roy McFadden

Widely admired as one of the most distinguished Ulster poets of his generation, Roy McFadden has been publishing poetry since before the Second World War. In the 1930s and 1940s he helped to promote Ulster writing by his co-editorship of *Rann, Ulster Voices,* and other periodicals; he also edited a series of poetry broadcasts for the BBC. His most recent collections – *Verifications* (1977) 'impressive in its rawness and energy' (Julian Symons, *Sunday Times*) and *A Watching Brief* (1979) – proved his ability to 'explore a local landscape, public and private, in subdued tones and modest measures'.

John Boyd has here selected the best of over forty years' work and coupled it with a section of new poems, including a remarkable sequence on Charles Dickens. A Belfast childhood, the War, the Troubles, a lifetime spent in the service of Justice; these and many other themes are laid out in precise, scrupulous, elegant verse.

'Without melodrama, he speaks in the accents of a man determined to get it right' – *Irish University Review*

'McFadden belongs to that honourable tradition of poets who may trace descent from Horace: fastidious word-carvers, urbane recorders of daily lives, followers of the golden mean. . . A quiet voice more audible than all the shriekers shrieking together.'
– *Irish Press*

'McFadden's language has the judiciously placing, probing action of a scalpel, uncontaminated by the materials it handles. . .' – *Stand*

£4.50
0 85640 282 6